SCHOLASTIC

25 Read & Write Mini-Books That Teach Phonics

BY NANCY I. SANDERS

NEW YORK • TORONTO • LONDON • AUCKLAND • SYDNEY
MEXICO CITY • NEW DELHI • HONG KONG • BUENOS AIRES

Teaching Resources

This book is dedicated to the Everett Free Library
in my hometown of Everett, Pennsylvania,
and all the librarians who lovingly devote
their time to foster an enjoyment of reading
in children of the community.

Cover design by Jason Robinson
Cover and interior artwork by Anne Kennedy
Interior design by Sydney Wright

ISBN: 0-439-45854-4

Printed in the U.S.A.

7 8 9 10 40 10 09 08 07 06 05

Contents

About This Book

How can teachers best help young children build the essential skills they need to learn to read? Techniques come and go for teaching the basics of reading to young children. But one thing remains—the necessity of understanding the relationship between the spoken sounds in a word and the letters used to represent those sounds. Having this basic comprehension greatly benefits students as they set out on their personal journey of learning to read.

In his book *Phonics from A to Z* (Scholastic, 1998), reading specialist Wiley Blevins identifies important areas of instruction that advance reading skills—automatic word recognition, comprehension of text, and development of a love of literature and a desire to read. Especially designed to support reading instruction, the stories in *25 Read & Write Mini-Books That Teach Phonics* can be valuable teaching tools you can use in the classroom.

As your students learn about sounds and their relationship with letters, they will begin to recognize and identify different phonetic groupings such as initial consonant blends, final consonants, and short vowels. Each of the 25 reproducible mini-books features a simple one-sentence story building on four key words from a homogenous phonetic grouping. For example, in the story *The Bear,* the words *bear, bike, baby,* and *ball* all share the initial consonant *b.* As children learn to identify the sound and spelling of initial consonant *b,* they can use this skill to decode the new word *bear.* When they follow each story's predictable pattern of homogenous phonetic groupings, they'll gain essential reading skills.

Accuracy in decoding words and an increased base of automatic word recognition are an integral part of each student's reading progress and fluency. From reading these mini-books, children will soon learn to recognize many words in the same phonetic groupings. The format of the mini-books adds to their appeal—they're just the right size for small hands and are easily tucked into a pocket to take anywhere. Children learn that reading is fun, and they'll set sail on a course charted for success.

Making the Mini-Books

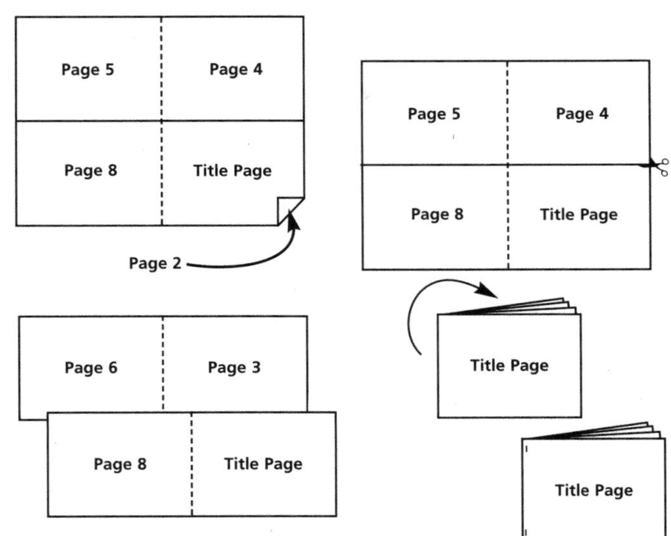

Follow these steps to copy and put together the mini-books.

- Remove the mini-book pages along the perforated lines. Make a double-sided copy on 8 1/2- by 11-inch paper.
- Cut the page in half along the solid line.
- Place page 3 behind the title page.
- Fold the pages in half along the dotted line. Check to be sure that the pages are in the proper order, and then staple them together along the book's spine.

NOTE: If you do not wish to make double-sided copies, you can photocopy single-sided copies of each page, cut apart the mini-pages, and stack them together in order, with the title page on top. Staple the pages together along the left-hand side.

Using the Mini-Books

The mini-books in this collection will spark the interest and enthusiasm of students, each one inspiring them to read another. Each mini-book tells a humorous one-sentence story that incorporates four key words that give practice in the same phonics skill. The books follow the same format and include illustrations to support young readers.

- The title page introduces children to the first word demonstrating the phonics skill—for example, *bear* for the initial consonant *b*.

- Pages 2 and 3 introduce the second key word in the sentence. Readers see how the word fits within that mini-book's featured phonetic grouping (initial consonant blends, final consonants, or short vowels, for example). Students can practice writing the word by tracing over the dotted lines of the grouping's letter(s).

- Pages 4 and 5 continue to the story, introducing and reinforcing a third key word (*baby*).
- Pages 6 and 7 introduce and reinforce the fourth key word (*ball*), and complete the story.

- Children can revisit the four key words on the back cover of each book by filling in the missing letters in the words to reinforce spelling.

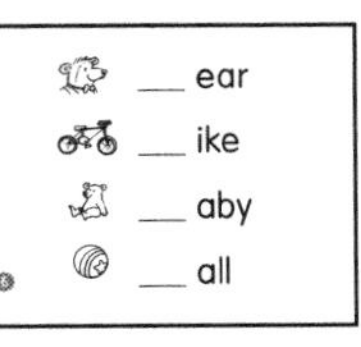

Activities to Extend Learning

Do You Hear What I Hear?

Pictures of animal ears help make this simple phonemic awareness game fun and engaging. Find a variety of animal pictures in magazines and calendars. Then, use the enlargement feature on a photocopier to make each animal's ears about 4 inches long. Cut out the ears and glue each one to a 5-inch square of tagboard for durability. Give an ear card to each student. Explain that you will read a list of words aloud slowly and you will ask children to listen for specific sounds within those words, such as final consonant *d*. (*mud, dad, maid, fan, bed, net, food*) Each time students hear that target sound, they are to hold up their individual ear card to let you know they heard it. If children hold up their ear cards at the wrong sound, ask them to listen for the sound again as you repeat the word.

Classroom Phonics Books

Take students on a vowel hunt in the classroom or another designated area. Tell children which vowel you are hunting for, such as long *a*. Then invite students to look for objects or pictures of items whose names contain that vowel sound. (*crate, gate, playground, raisins, staple, tape*) After every child finds a word, have each student write the word he or she found and draw a picture of it on a large index card. Collect the index cards and turn them into a class book. Label the cover page with the corresponding vowel sound. For each new sound introduced to students, embark on a new hunt and make a new class book. Make these phonics books available for browsing during free time and at Open House.

In Grandma's Suitcase

Imagine Grandma's coming! What will she bring in her suitcase? Bring to school a small suitcase filled with items or pictures of objects that contain the target sound, such as initial consonant blend *cl-*. (*clam, clock, cloud, clover, claw, cliff, clown, cloth, clip, clothes*) Review the items with students. When finished, pack up the suitcase and play a simple game. Begin the game by saying, "In her suitcase, Grandma brought a *clock*." Ask volunteers to repeat the name of the item and add another item with the same target sound. The first volunteer may say, "In her suitcase, Grandma brought a *clock* and a *clown*." Continue the game until the class has an extensive list of words containing the target sound.

Short-Vowel Game

Divide a 3-foot sheet of butcher paper into five equal sections. Write one vowel on each section, setting up a grid of letters. Invite students to take turns tossing a cotton ball onto the paper. Ask, "Where did your cotton ball land?" Have children name the letter and then say a word that contains the short-vowel sound. For more phonics fun, vary the game using different target sounds, such as final consonants or initial consonant blends.

Phonics Activity Cards

Make multiple copies of the word cards on pages 8 through 14. (These are the 100 words introduced in the mini-books.) Cut them apart and use them for a variety of activities. Here are some suggestions.

✳ **Spin the Wheel** Make a wheel-shaped spinner by drawing a large circle on a 6-inch piece of tagboard. Divide the circle into five sections. Label each section with a different initial consonant blend, such as *cl-*, *dr-*, *fl-*, *sn-*, and *sw-*. Then cut out an arrow shape from tagboard and mount it with a brass fastener to the center, creating a spinner. To make sturdy word cards, glue each card containing an initial consonant blend to a small index card and laminate for durability. (You can play this game with any of the five sets of word cards—simply make a spinner for each phonics skill.)

Here's how to play the game:

- Select four sets of initial consonant words cards. (You can make four copies of a set from one story. Or, you can use sets from four different stories.) Shuffle and distribute the cards to players. (This activity works best with a group of four children.)
- Have players lay their cards faceup in front of them.
- The first player takes a turn spinning the wheel and announces to the group where the arrow landed. ("The arrow landed on *sn-*.")
- If the first player has a word card with that initial consonant blend, he or she places the word card next to the spinner (creating a stack of discarded cards). If the player does not have a card with that initial consonant blend, play continues with the next child.
- The game ends when all players have discarded every card.

✳ **Our Phonics Box** Wrap an empty shoe box and its lid with butcher paper, as you would a present. Cut a 1- by 6-inch opening in the lid for a mail slot. Glue a set of word cards that match the phonics skills you are teaching to the butcher paper wrapping. If students are working on initial consonant *b*, you might use the word cards from the story *The Bear.* (*bear, bike, baby, ball*) Then write "Initial Consonant *B*" on the shoe box's lid. When the phonics box is ready, put a basket with pencils and index cards beside it. All week, invite children to write words that have that initial consonant on index cards and slip them through the mail slot. On Friday, open the shoe box and review the words with students. Encourage children to read and examine the words during free time. Use the box again to focus on a different phonics skill.

✳ **Short Vowels Classroom Banner** On construction paper, draw five different types of clothing (for example: shirts, pants, boots, mittens, and hats). Cut out four copies of each type of clothing. Divide the class into five groups. Give the first group four paper shirts and four short-*a* word cards. Give the second group four paper pants and four short-*e* word cards, and so on. Have children glue one word card on each piece of paper clothing and write the target letter. Then, use spring-type clothespins to create a banner. Clip each piece of clothing onto a length of clothesline. Invite groups of students to take turns adding different sets of word cards to the clothesline. Encourage children to use the banner as they would a word wall, to strengthen spelling skills and support vocabulary development.

* **Our Garden of Final Consonants** Grow a phonics garden! Cover a bulletin board with craft paper. On the board, write the title "Our Garden of Final Consonants" in large, colorful letters. Mount five tall sunflowers with green stems and yellow flowers. On each flower, write one final consonant. Then cut out green paper leaves, one for each student. Give each child a leaf, a word card containing a final consonant, and a red crayon. As a class, discuss and identify the final consonant. Have children trace the final consonants on their word card with the red crayon, and glue the word card on the leaf. Invite students to tape their leaves to the corresponding sunflower, giving each flower stem four leaves. As you introduce other phonics skills, modify the flowers or scene to suit your needs.

* **Initial Consonants Pocket Chart** Write "Initial Consonants" on a sentence strip and put it in the top of a pocket chart. To make labeled categories for the chart, write the following consonants on separate sentence strips: *b-*, *f-*, *l-*, *m-*, *t-*. Put each label in a separate row of the pocket chart. Explain that students will match each word card to one of the initial consonants in the pocket chart. Then, distribute the initial consonant word cards randomly to children. Invite one volunteer at a time to place his or her word card in the correct row of the chart. To extend this activity, consider inviting each volunteer to say another word with the same beginning sound.

* **Reading Journals** Use file folders to create reading journals. Begin by writing the following headings on separate sheets of white paper: *b-*, *f-*, *l-*, *m-*, *t-*, *cl-*, *dr-*, *fl-*, *sn-*, *sw-*, *-d*, *-l*, *-t*, *-mp*, *-nt*, long *a*, long *e*, long *i*, long *o*, long *u*, short *a*, short *e*, short *i*, short *o*, and short *u*. Use a photocopier to make a phonetic-grouping set for each student. To make the journals, staple each set to the inside of an open file folder. Distribute the folders to children. Then, give each student a copy of any one of the pages from 8 through 14. Have children cut apart the words and sort them into separate phonetic groups. As a class, discuss the strategies students used to sort the words. When ready, have children glue the word cards to the corresponding journal pages. Encourage students to pair off and practice reading their journals aloud to each other. When the journals contain all of the 100 word cards, have children take their journals home to share with families.

Word Cards

bear	baby
bike	ball

farmer	monkey
fast	mommy
field	money
fair	mall
lamb	turtle
lion	turkey
lunch	tag
lake	toes

clown	fly
clothes	flea
climb	flutes
cliff	flowers
dragon	snail
drink	snake
dress	snack
dream	snow

swan	seal
sweater	pail
swing	meal
swims	tail
kid	goat
road	cat
toad	boat
mud	rat

chimp	ape
camp	snake
jump	race
ramp	cake
ant	bee
plant	tree
paint	eat
tent	ice cream

mice	mule
dive	music
bikes	bugle
write	cube
mole	bat
robe	mask
nose	cat
rose	grass

Ted	fox
elf	top
sled	box
shelf	pop
fish	duck
swim	bug
dish	bus
Kim	rug

The Bear

___ ear

___ ike

___ aby

___ all

The bear
on the bike
has a baby . . .

baby

2

The bear
on the bike . . .

3

bike

6

The bear
on the bike
has a baby
and a ball.

7

ball

The Farmer

The farmer
ran very fast
on the field...

field

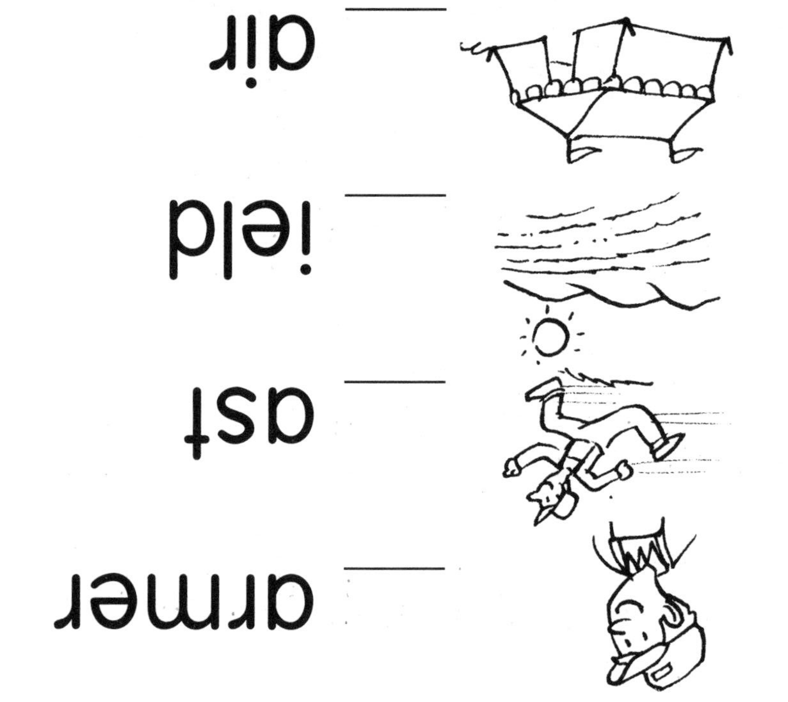

__ armer

__ ast

__ ield

__ air

7

fair

2

The farmer
ran very fast...

6

The farmer
ran very fast
on the field
at the fair.

3

fast

The Lamb

amb ____

ion ____

unch ____

ake ____

The lamb
and the lion
eat their lunch . . .

_unch

2

The lamb
and the lion...

lion

3

The lamb
and the lion
eat their lunch
at the lake.

6

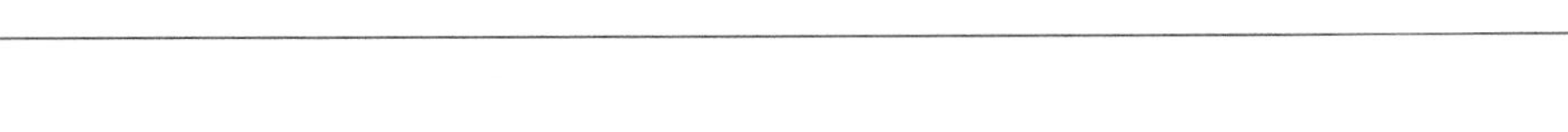

lake

7

A Monkey

A monkey
and her mommy
spend some money...

25 Read & Write Mini-Books That Teach Phonics Scholastic Teaching Resources

m oney

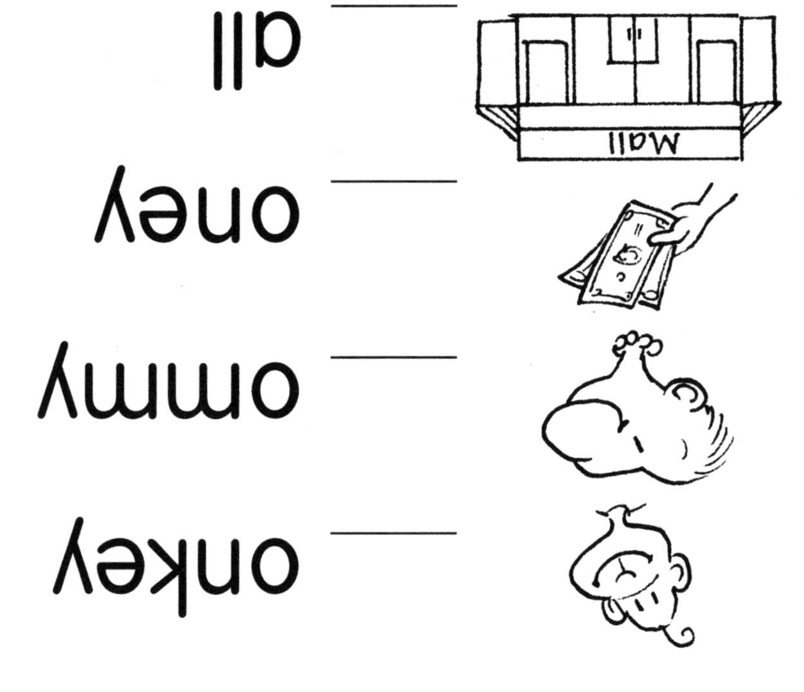

___ onkey

___ ommy

___ oney

___ all

7

mall

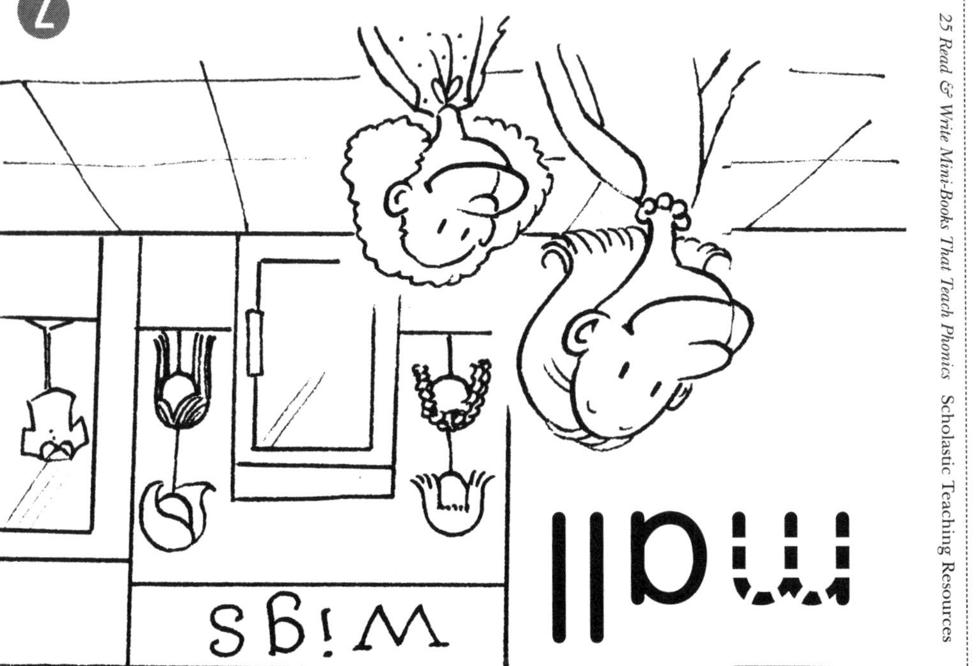

2

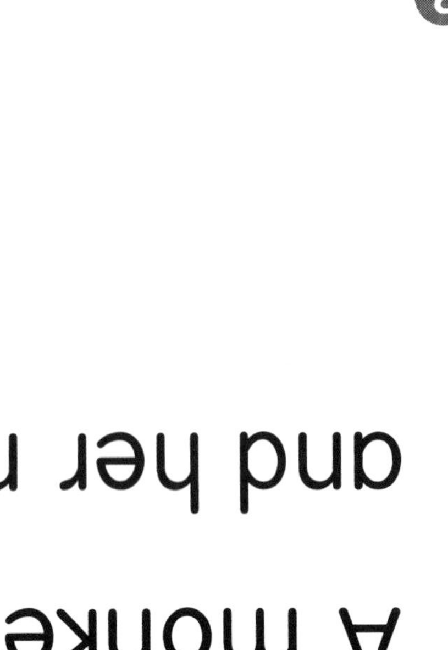

A monkey
and her mommy...

A monkey
and her mommy
spend some money
at the mall.

6

mommy

3

A Turtle

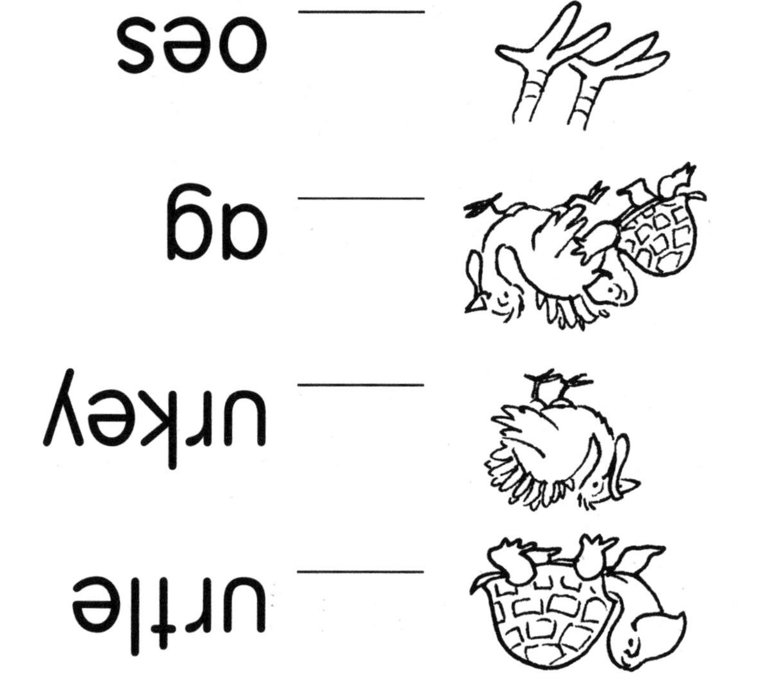

__ urtle

__ urkey

__ ag

__ oes

8

A turtle
and a turkey
play tag...

4

_ag

5

A turtle

and a turkey...

2

toes

7

turkey

3

A turtle

and a turkey

play tag

on their toes.

6

A Clown

8

__ __ own

__ __ othes

__ __ imb

__ __ iff

A clown
in silly clothes
wants to climb...

4

climb

5

7

cliff

2

A clown
in silly clothes...

A clown
in silly clothes
wants to climb
up the cliff.

6

clothes

3

A Dragon

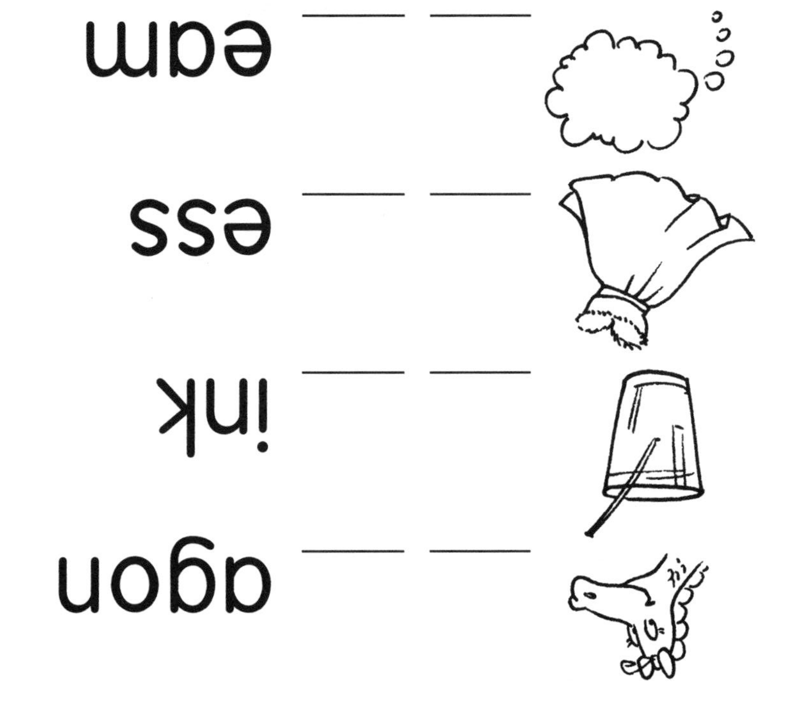

A dragon dropped her drink on her dress...

A dragon
dropped her drink...

drink

A dragon
dropped her drink
on her dress
in a dream.

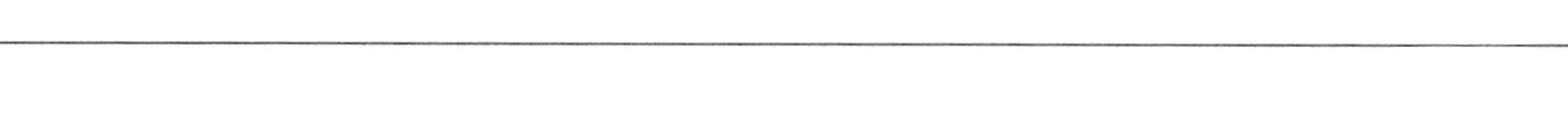

25 Read & Write Mini-Books That Teach Phonics Scholastic Teaching Resources

dream

The Fly

The fly

and the flea

played their flutes...

flutes

__ __ y

__ __ ea

__ __ utes

__ __ owers

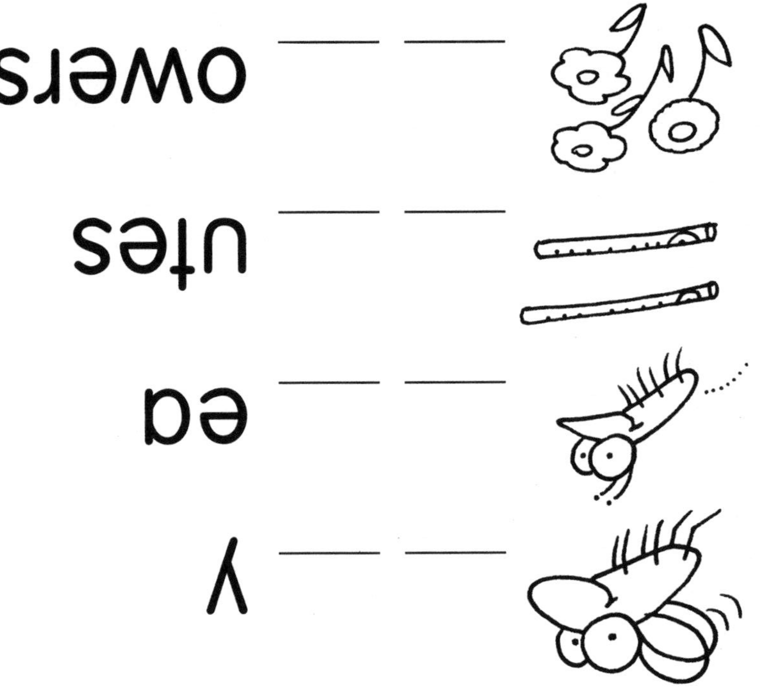

The fly
and the flea...

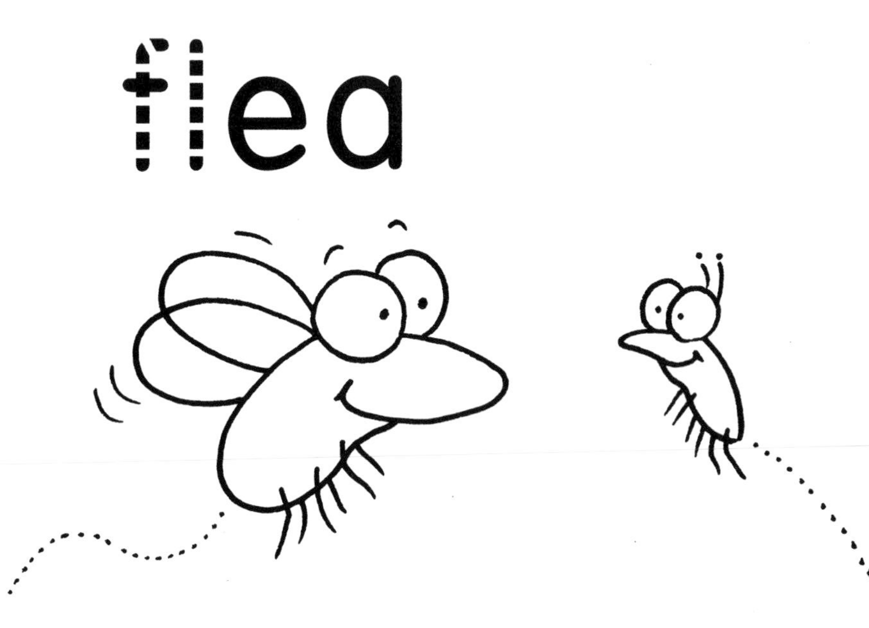

flea

3

The fly
and the flea
played their flutes
on the flowers.

6

flowers

7

The Snail

The snail
and the snake
eat a snack...

4

snack

5

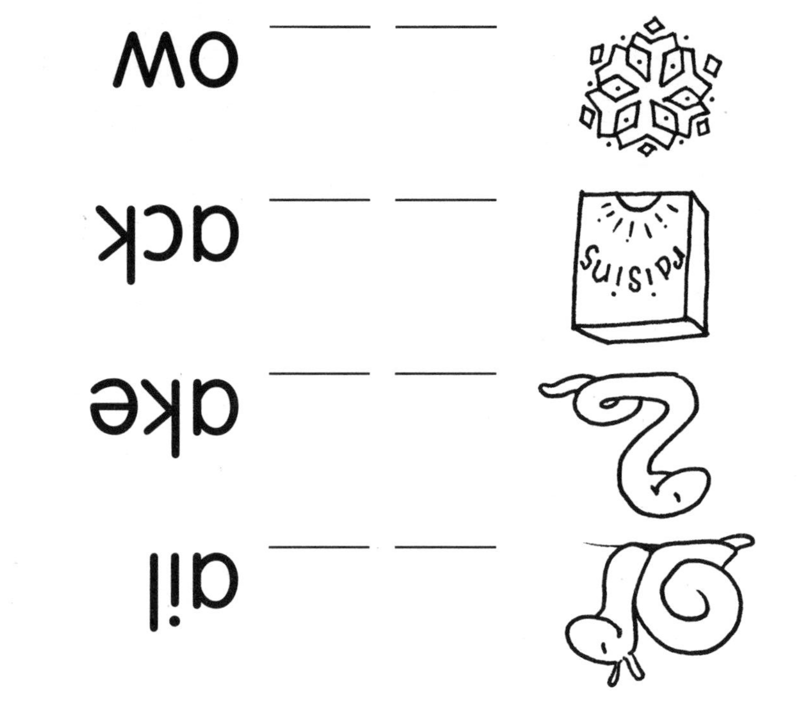

__ __ ail

__ __ ake

__ __ ack

__ __ ow

8

7

snow

25 *Read & Write Mini-Books That Teach Phonics* Scholastic Teaching Resources

2

The snail
and the snake...

The snail
and the snake
eat a snack
in the snow.

6

snake

3

A swan
in a sweater
likes to swing...

swing

A Swan

__ __ an
__ __ eater
__ __ ing
__ __ ims

2

A swan

in a sweater...

3

sweater

6

A swan

in a sweater

likes to swing

when it swims.

7

swims

25 Read & Write Mini-Books That Teach Phonics   Scholastic Teaching Resources

A Kid

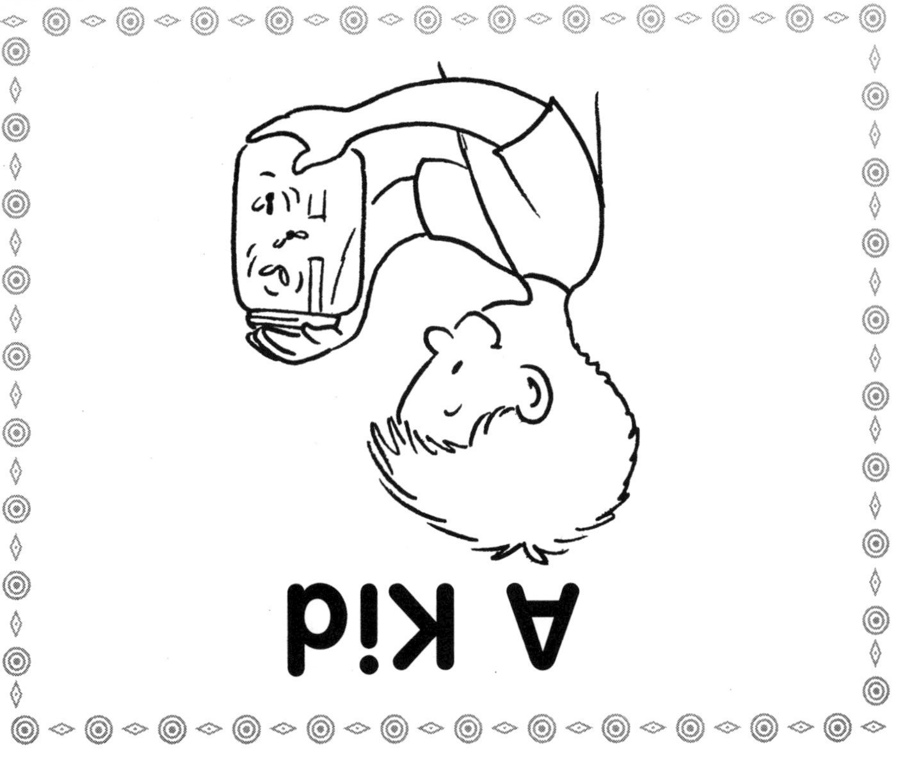

ki ___

roa ___

toa ___

mu ___

A kid

on the road

saw a toad...

25 Read & Write Mini-Books That Teach Phonics Scholastic Teaching Resources

toad

7

mud

2

A kid
on the road...

6

A kid
on the road
saw a toad
in the mud.

3

road

A Seal

sea ___

pai ___

mea ___

tai ___

A seal
with a pail
eats a meal . . .

mea ___!

Seal
seal food

A seal
with a pail . . .

pail

A seal
with a pail
eats a meal
on its tail.

tail

The Goat

8

goa___

ca___

boa___

ra___

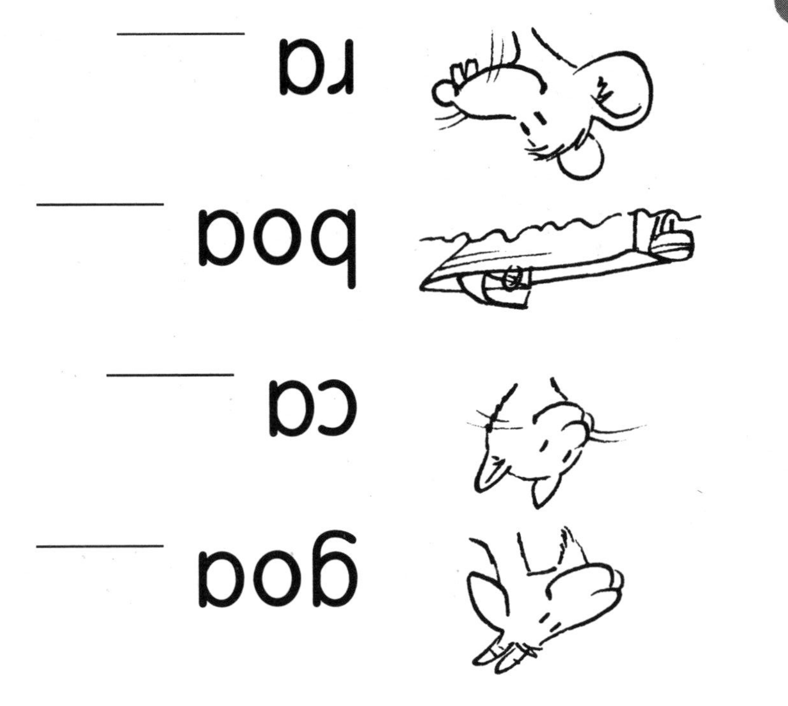

The goat
and the cat
ride in a boat...

4

25 Read & Write Mini-Books That Teach Phonics Scholastic Teaching Resources

boat

5

2

The goat

and the cat...

3

cat

6

The goat

and the cat

ride in a boat

that pulls a rat.

7

rat

A Chimp

chi__ __

ca__ __

ju__ __

ra__ __

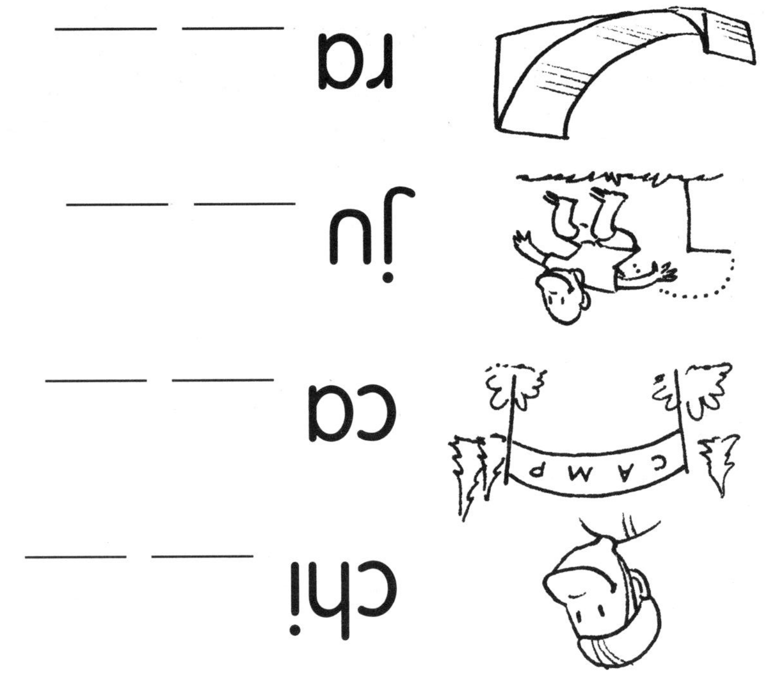

A chimp
at the camp
took a jump...

jump

25 Read & Write Mini-Books That Teach Phonics Scholastic Teaching Resources

ramp

7

A chimp
at the camp...

A chimp
at the camp
took a jump
off the ramp.

6

camp

3

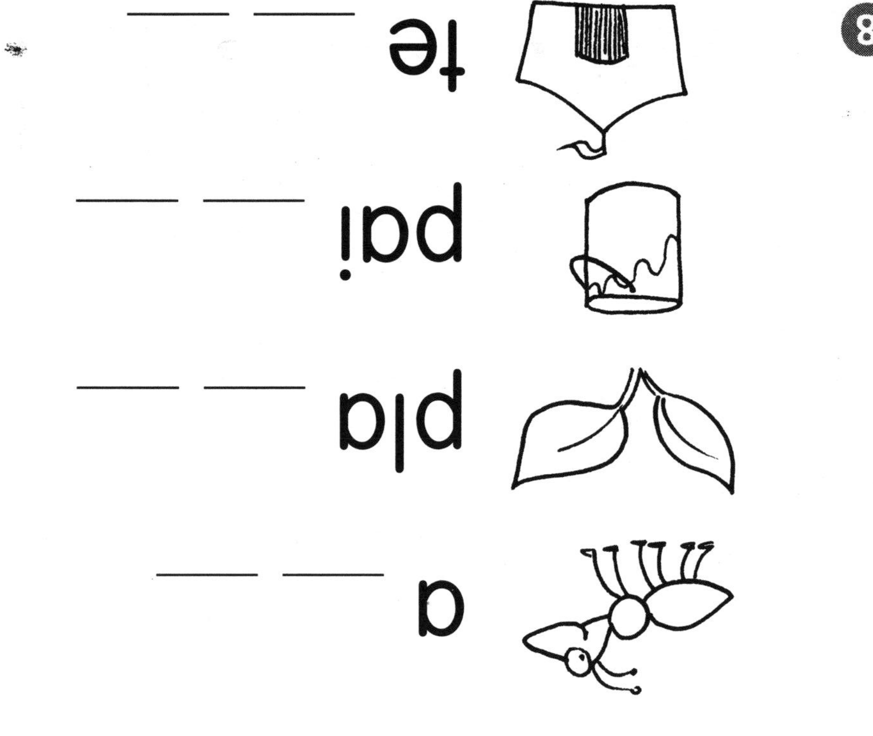

The ant
on the plant
likes to paint...

The ant
on the plant...

2

tent

7

plant

3

The ant
on the plant
likes to paint
the big tent.

6

The Ape

8

___pe

sn___ke

r___ce

c___ke

The ape
and the snake
had a race...

4

race

5

2

The ape
and the snake...

3

snake

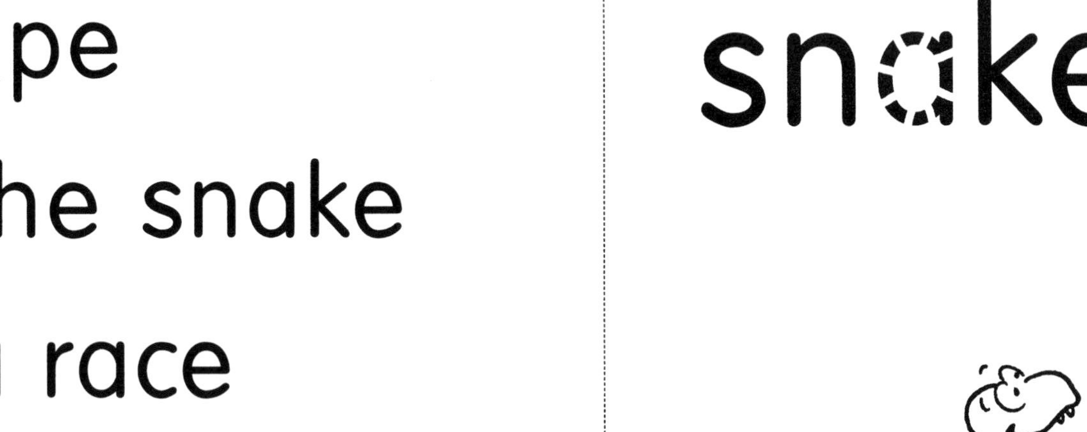

6

The ape
and the snake
had a race
to eat cake.

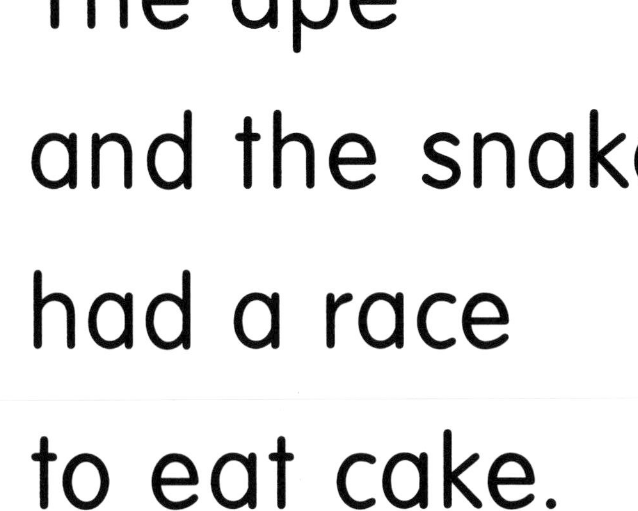

7

cake

The Bee

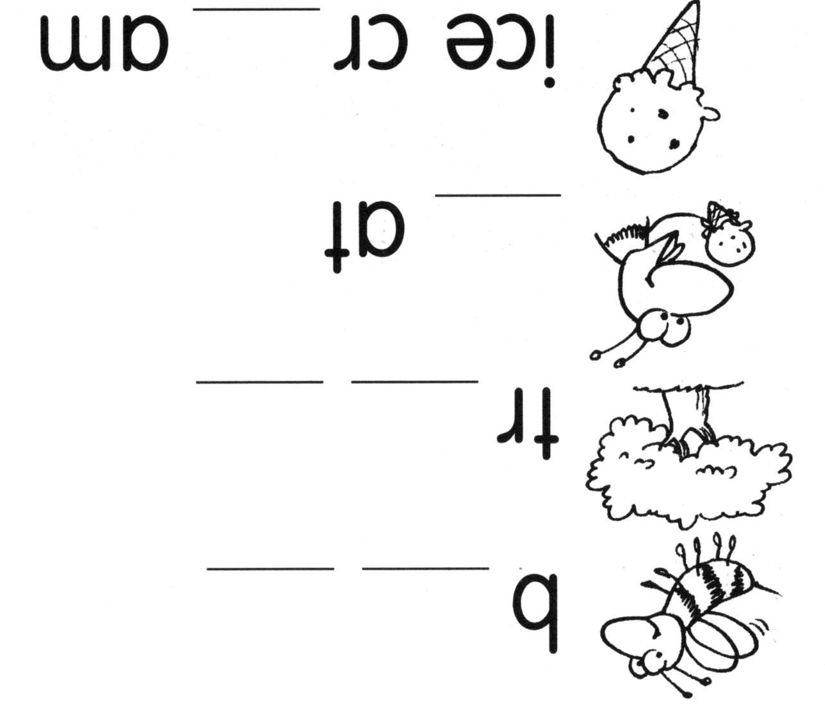

b__ __

tr__ __

__at

ice cr__am

The bee
on the tree
likes to eat...

25 Read & Write Mini-Books That Teach Phonics Scholastic Teaching Resources

eat

The bee
on the tree . . .

The bee
on the tree
likes to eat
cold ice cream.

tree

m ___ ce

d ___ ve

b ___ kes

wr ___ te

The mice

who can dive

and ride bikes...

25 Read & Write Mini-Books That Teach Phonics Scholastic Teaching Resources

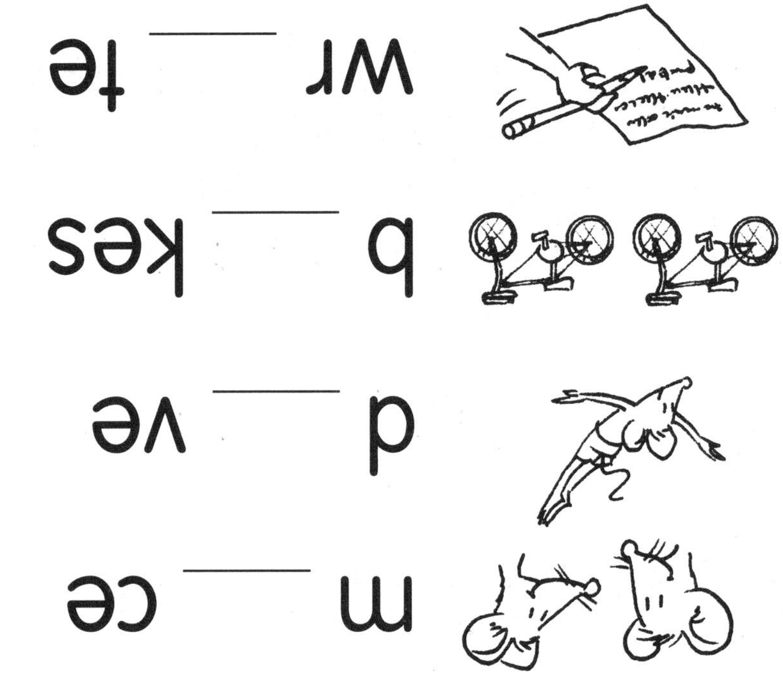

The mice
who can dive…

dive

3

The mice
who can dive
and ride bikes
like to write.

6

write

7

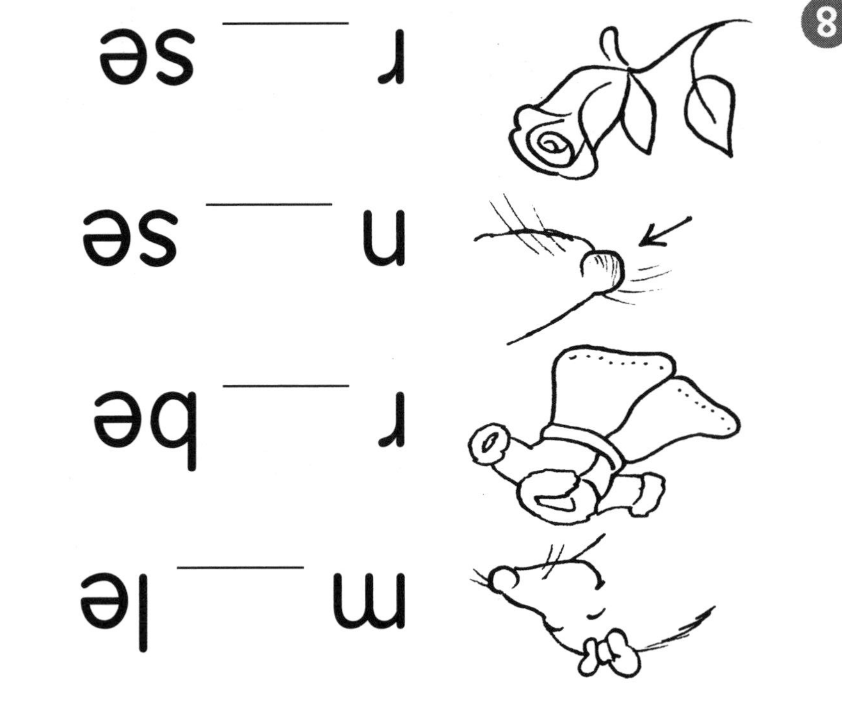

8

A mole
in a robe
put her nose . . .

4

5

A mole
in a robe...

robe

rose

A mole
in a robe
put her nose
in a rose.

The Mule

m___le
m___sic
b___gle
c___be

8

The mule
who likes music
plays the bugle . . .

bugle

5

2

The mule

who likes music...

cube

7

3

music

The mule

who likes music

plays the bugle

on a cube.

6

The Bat

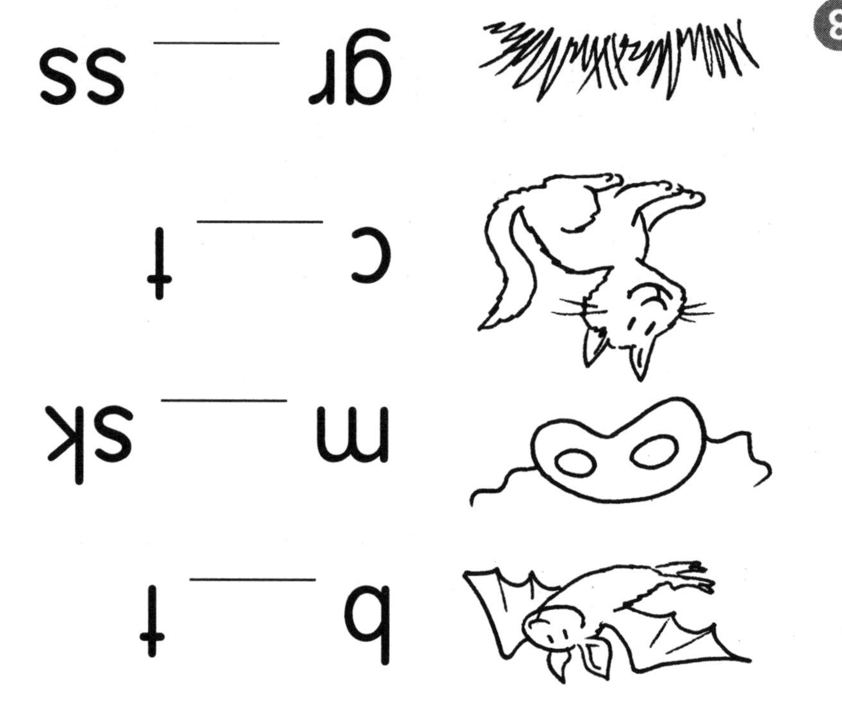

b __ t

m __ sk

c __ t

gr __ ss

The bat
with the mask
put a cat...

cat

2

The bat
with the mask...

3

mask

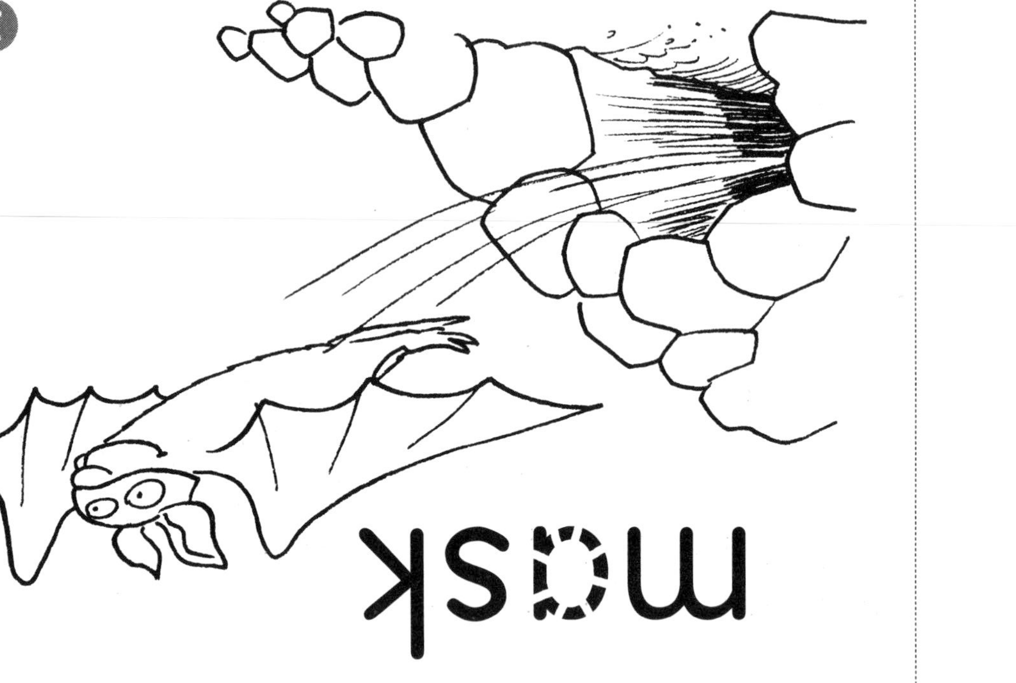

6

The bat
with the mask
put a cat
on the grass.

7

grass

Ted
put the elf
on a sled...

sled

25 Read & Write Mini-Books That Teach Phonics Scholastic Teaching Resources

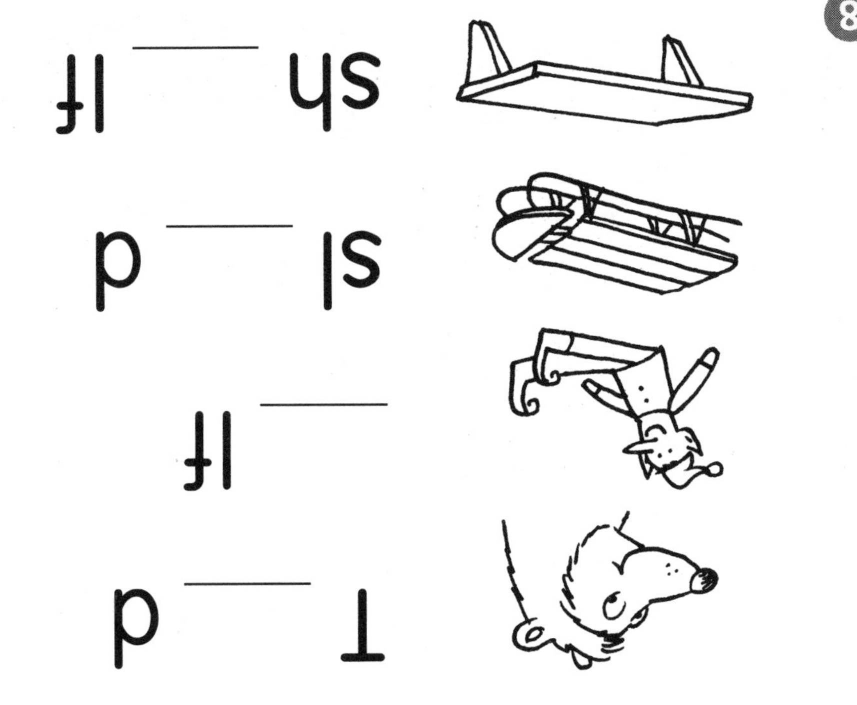

T __ d

__ lf

sl __ d

sh __ lf

Ted

Ted
put the elf...

elf

Ted
put the elf
on a sled
on the shelf.

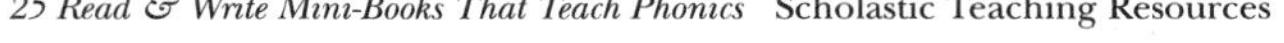

shelf

A fish
likes to swim
in a dish...

dish

A Fish

f ___ sh

sw ___ m

d ___ sh

K ___ m

2

A fish
likes to swim . . .

3

swim

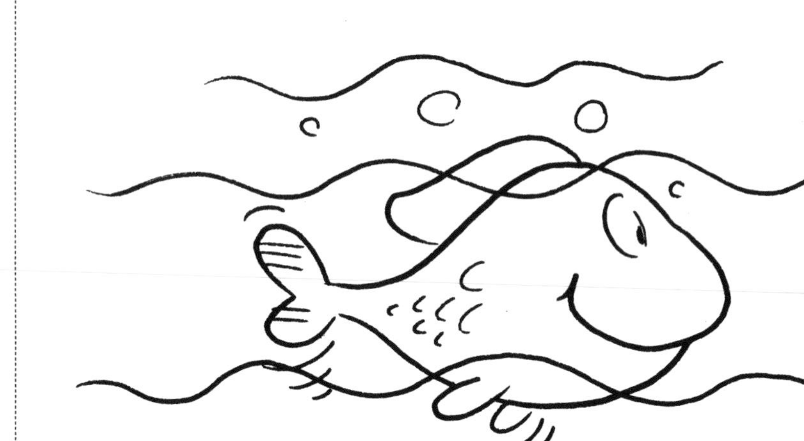

6

A fish
likes to swim
in a dish
held by Kim.

7

Kim

The fox

saw the top

of a box...

b○x

The Fox

f ___ x

t ___ p

b ___ x

p ___ p

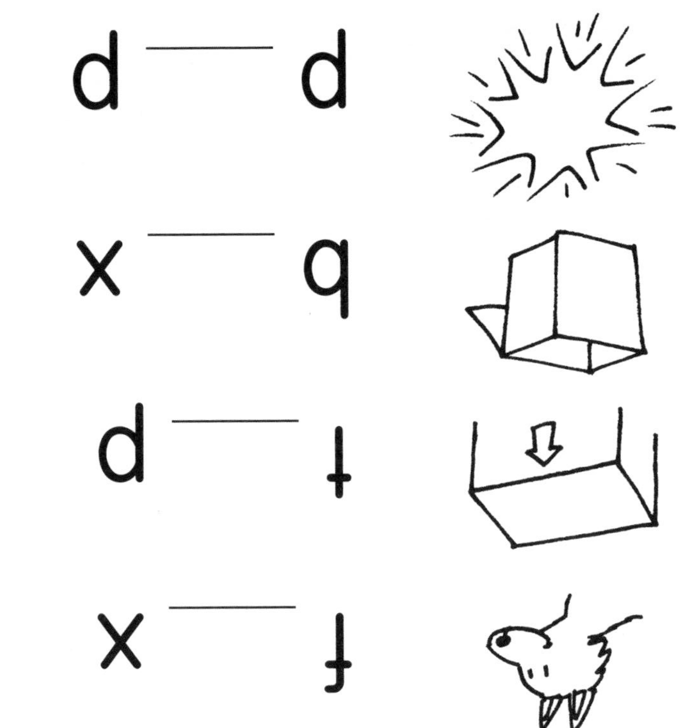

2

The fox
saw the top...

3

top

6

The fox
saw the top
of a box
that went pop!

7

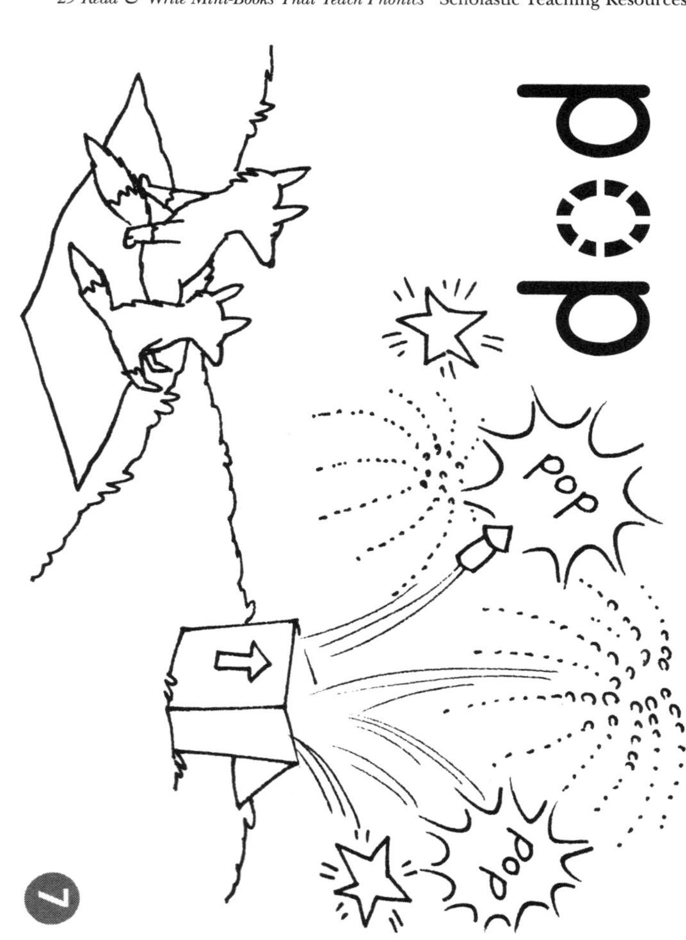

pop

A Duck

d __ ck

b __ g

b __ s

r __ g

A duck
and a bug
drive the bus...

bus

2

A duck
and a bug . . .

3

bug

6

A duck
and a bug
drive the bus
on the rug.

7

rug